W9-DEB-926

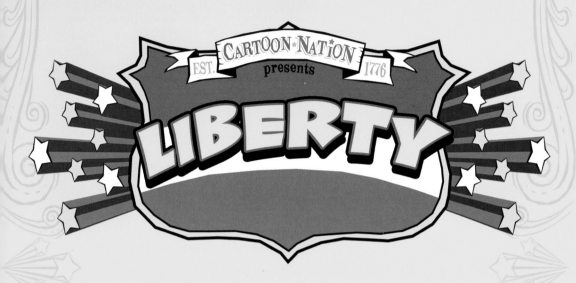

CARTOON ★ NATION presents

EST. 1776

LIBERTY

by Terry Collins

illustrated by Brian Bascle

CONSULTANT:
Michael Bailey
Colonel William J. Walsh Associate Professor
of American Government
Georgetown University, Washington, D.C.

Capstone press®

Mankato, Minnesota

Graphic Library is published by Capstone Press,
151 Good Counsel Drive, P.O. Box 669, Mankato, Minnesota 56002.
www.capstonepress.com

1 2 3 4 5 6 14 13 12 11 10 09

Library of Congress Cataloging-in-Publication Data
Collins, Terry.
    Liberty / by Terry Collins; illustrated by Brian Bascle.
    p. cm. — (Graphic library. Cartoon nation)
    Includes bibliographical references and index.
    Summary: "In cartoon format, explains the concept of liberty and describes how the
pursuit of liberty has shaped the United States" — Provided by the publisher.
    ISBN-13: 978-1-4296-2340-7 (hardcover)
    ISBN-10: 1-4296-2340-3 (hardcover)
    1. Liberty — Juvenile literature. 2. Civil rights — United States — Juvenile literature.
3. United States — History — Juvenile literature. I. Bascle, Brian, ill. II. Title.
JC585.C437 2009
323.440973 — dc22   2008029655

Set Designer
Bob Lentz

Book Designer
Alison Thiele

Cover Artist
Kelly Brown

Editor
Christopher L. Harbo

Editor's note: Direct quotations from primary sources are indicated by a yellow background.

Direct quotations appear on the following pages:
Page 4, from the U.S. Code Online Web site, *Title 4 — Flag and Seal, Seat of Government,
    and the States, Section 4*, http://www.access.gpo.gov/uscode/uscmain.html.
Page 14, from *Jean-Jacques Rousseau: The Social Contract*, translated by Maurice Cranston
    (New York: Penguin Books, 1968).
Page 23, from United Nations Web site. *The Universal Declaration of Human Rights*,
    http://www.unhchr.ch/udhr/lang/eng.htm.
Page 27, from Packard Humanities Institute Web site. *The Papers of Benjamin Franklin,
    Volume 6, Pennsylvania Assembly: Reply to the Governor, Tuesday, November 11, 1755*,
    http://www.franklinpapers.org/franklin/framedVolumes.jsp.

TABLE OF CONTENTS

★ Pledging Allegiance **4**

★ The Liberty Trio............................ **6**

★ When in Rome **8**

★ Stuck in the Middle **10**

★ Join or Die **12**

★ They Came from France................. **14**

★ The Bill of Rights **16**

★ Liberty for All............................ **18**

★ Liberty Enlightening the World **20**

★ The Four Freedoms...................... **22**

★ A Lack of Liberty **24**

★ Liberty Lost?............................. **26**

Time Line 28
Glossary... 30
Read More 30
Internet Sites.................................. 31
Index 31
                                               32

Every morning in classrooms across America, students stand up. They place their right hands over their hearts. Everyone faces the flag and says the following words:

I pledge allegiance to the Flag of the United States of America, and to the Republic for which it stands, one Nation under God, indivisible, with liberty and justice for all.

What are you doing?

I'm doing like the pledge says and making myself invisible.

indivisible — not able to be divided or broken into pieces

Not invisible — indivisible!

Americans know the Pledge of Allegiance, but do they understand what the words mean? What is "liberty and justice for all"? Most people know that justice is fairness. When a law is broken, the guilty are punished. Liberty is harder to define, but it's much more than a famous statue.

The definition of liberty is similar to that of freedom. In America, liberty grants citizens freedom from unfair or one-sided government control. Political liberty gives people freedom to exercise their rights as guaranteed by law.

People who live in a free society celebrate liberty in several ways. For example, they are able to practice the religion of their choice. They may talk about any subject without fear of being arrested. They are also free to read books on any subject they choose.

Where do you think you're going?

To the movies. I'm going to enjoy my liberty!

Nice try, Bobby.

ANARCHY

Actually, liberty without some limits is anarchy. Free countries have laws for the people. You can't steal things or hurt others. These laws protect the rights of everyone. Liberty comes with a price. Americans are willing to pay that price to hold on to their personal freedoms.

Across the world, the three basic kinds of liberty are political, social, and economic. Americans receive these liberties at birth. While all liberties guarantee freedoms, they also come with limits.

POLITICAL!   SOCIAL!   ECONOMIC!

Political liberty gives people the right to vote. People can join the political party of their choice. They can criticize the government without fear. Citizens offer their thoughts on the political process. And they can run for public office.

Who are you voting for in the election?

I'm voting for me!

Social liberty includes many rights that Americans use daily. These rights include freedom of speech, religion, and assembly.

One of the most important of these freedoms is the ability to practice free speech. This liberty gives the right to express opinions openly. Freedom of speech allows people to talk without fear of being arrested.

Economic liberty allows Americans to make choices about money. They can invest it, save it in a bank, or spend their earnings. This right also lets qualified people choose the job of their choice.

I also have the right to expect a decent tip!

ROAD TO LIBERTY

The basic concept of liberty dates back thousands of years to ancient Rome. While today's citizens of the United States take liberty for granted, the road to earning these rights was not simple. Getting and keeping liberty took a long time.

More than 2,500 years ago, the people of ancient Rome believed in *libertas*, or liberty. But liberty for all, while a good idea, was driven by social class. Only the rich upper classes truly enjoyed freedom as understood by today's society.

How long is this job going to take?

Hey, Rome wasn't built in a day, you know!

class — a group of people in society with a similar way of life or range of income

Neither was liberty.

Slaves were even worse off than the lower classes. Slaves were considered property. They had no legal rights. Ancient Romans saw liberty as something to be given or acquired. No one was born free.

So which do you want – the vase or the slave?

Like you could ever put a price on human life!

YE OLDE YARD SALE

PRICE REDUCED MUST GO

Liberty was a privilege granted by the laws of Rome.
Slaves gained their liberty only under certain conditions.
When a slave was set free, his master held a ceremony.

You are now liberated! Enjoy your freedom.

Thanks! Um, know anyone who's hiring former slaves?

GODDESS OF LIBERTY

Libertas was the Roman goddess of personal freedom. Temples were built in her honor. She was shown on coins and in artwork. Libertas wore a wreath and carried a spear. She also wore a felt cap known as a pileus. Slaves were given a pileus when they were freed.

Even after being freed, many former slaves had to return to their old master's service for several days a year. They were expected to uphold the laws of Rome. Slaves who did not follow these rules could be enslaved again.

So much for liberty.

With the fall of the Roman empire in 476, the Middle Ages began. Europe was split into areas ruled by kings. Rich nobles served royal families. Poor peasants had no money and no rights.

> What happened to my liberty, anyway?

Some of these peasants were also known as serfs. They worked the lands owned by the nobles. In return, serfs received food and shelter. The nobles kept the profits of the farmlands and paid taxes to the king.

> The more things change, the more they stay the same. Am I right?

This political system lasted until 1215. That year, English nobles drafted the Magna Carta. This document created laws for all men to obey. These laws stopped the king from abusing his royal powers.

Okay, I promise, no more taxes without talking it over with you guys first.

The Magna Carta put many liberties into law. It also protected the rights of the king's subjects.

- The king could not create new taxes without the agreement of his nobles.
- No free man could be put in prison, banned from the country, or have his property taken unless allowed by the law.
- The ideas of no taxation without a voice in government, respecting a person's legal rights, and trial by jury came from the Magna Carta.
- The Magna Carta established the idea that even a king had to obey the law, just like everyone else.

What's a king got to do to get a table around here?

THE ENGLISH BILL OF RIGHTS

In 1689, the English Bill of Rights established even more rights and liberties for the British people. This bill also cut many of the king's powers. All of these changes brought Britain closer to becoming a democracy.

In the 1700s, American colonies were ready to end British rule. King George III had to limit taxes in Great Britain. But there was nothing to stop him from forcing American colonists to pay more. He taxed stamps, newspapers, and even tea. These unfair taxes led to the Revolutionary War in 1775.

What else can we tax? Ooh, I know! Let's tax baseball!

Great idea. The tax will start as soon as the game is invented.

Philadelphia leader Benjamin Franklin published a cartoon asking American colonists to combine forces against outside enemies. The cartoon showed the American colonies as a snake cut into pieces. The message was simple. Unless the colonists joined together, they would never win their liberty.

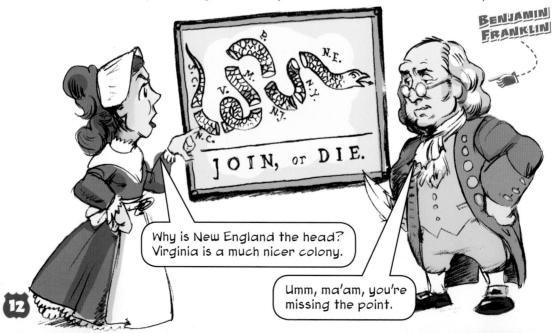

Why is New England the head? Virginia is a much nicer colony.

Umm, ma'am, you're missing the point.

Virginia lawyer Thomas Jefferson was chosen to write the Declaration of Independence. The document said that all 13 colonies were free and independent states. The Declaration was presented to the Second Continental Congress on June 28, 1776.

THOMAS JEFFERSON

I think the word "liberty" only has one letter "t."

Aw, go fly a kite, Franklin!

The Continental Congress revised and approved the Declaration in Philadelphia on July 4, 1776. As president of the Congress, John Hancock was the first to sign it.

JOHN HANCOCK

Anyone got a pen?

John Hancock to the rescue!

As the Declaration said, colonists were ready for the rights of life, liberty, and the pursuit of happiness.

CREATIVE INSPIRATION

In 1689, the English philosopher John Locke wrote *Two Treatises of Government*. The book noted that any government must protect the liberty of its citizens. If liberty was not protected, then the citizens should revolt. Locke's words inspired Thomas Jefferson while writing the Declaration of Independence.

THEY CAME FROM FRANCE

During the 1700s, three Frenchmen wrote about the liberties that should be given to all people. The first was a writer and thinker named Charles Montesquieu. He had the idea of the separation of government powers into three separate branches. His book, *The Spirit of the Laws*, influenced James Madison, the "Father of the U.S. Constitution."

JAMES MADISON

Montesquieu says government should be set up so that no man need be afraid of another. What do you think?

WEE THB PEOPLE

Goo!

JEAN-JACQUES ROUSSEAU

The second writer was Jean-Jacques Rousseau. Rousseau wrote several books. The most important of these was *The Social Contract*. In this book, Rousseau said that any government draws power from the people. He urged cooperation between all men.

Man is born free, and everywhere he is in chains.

THREE BRANCHES OF GOVERNMENT

The U.S. Constitution is designed for executive, legislative, and judicial branches of government to work together. These three branches are united through a system of checks and balances. One branch can change or veto decisions of another branch to keep the branch from gaining too much power. In America, the president, Congress, and the courts are equal.

The third writer was a man named Voltaire. He didn't like politicians interfering with the rights of the people. Voltaire wrote more than 2,000 books and pamphlets. *The Philosophical Dictionary* was his most controversial work. To protect his safety, the witty Voltaire denied writing the book.

Voltaire? Never heard of him.

CHEZ VOLTAIRE

VOLTAIRE LIVES HERE

VOLTAIRE

I hope this doesn't mess up my hair!

The French people listened to these writers. In 1789, their books led people to overthrow the monarchy. The rights of the people were not being respected. Four years later, France's King Louis XVI and Queen Marie Antoinette were sent to the guillotine. For withholding liberty from their people, they paid with their lives.

monarchy — a system of government in which the ruler is a king or queen

MARIE ANTOINETTE

THE BILL OF RIGHTS

In 1788, the new American government split power between Congress, the courts, and the president. But some basic liberties were lacking in the final draft of the Constitution.

I know we were done, but I think we need to add a few things.

JAMES MADISON

In 1791, 10 amendments were added to the Constitution. They guaranteed essential liberties for all citizens. These amendments are known as the Bill of Rights. They limit the powers of the government, while protecting the rights of all Americans.

1ST AMENDMENT

Allows you to speak freely and get your news from a free press. It also lets you practice a religion of your choice and gather in groups peacefully.

2ND AMENDMENT

Gives you the right to keep and bear weapons in a safe and secure manner to protect yourself.

3RD AMENDMENT

Promises that you will never have to let soldiers live in your home or eat your food.

4TH AMENDMENT

Protects you and your property from unlawful searches.

5TH AMENDMENT

Promises you a fair trial in court. The amendment also ensures that the government will pay you a fair price if it wants to buy your land.

6TH AMENDMENT

Gives you the right to a jury trial. Also, you must be told of the charges against you.

7TH AMENDMENT

Allows a jury to decide trials involving money. The jury also decides how much money will be paid in damages.

8TH AMENDMENT

Promises that punishment will fit the crime. You can't get life in prison for driving through a red light.

9TH AMENDMENT

Protects and respects all of your rights, even if they aren't listed in the Bill of Rights.

10TH AMENDMENT

Limits the federal government's powers to those granted in the Constitution. That way, state governments can keep their own local laws, as long as they don't break federal laws.

The early 1800s brought new freedoms to Americans, but the practice of slavery continued. A country founded on liberty could not allow the ownership of another human being to continue.

Don't worry. Liberty will find you, too.

Slavery tore the country apart. The battle over the Southern states' right to keep slaves led to the Civil War in 1861. More than 600,000 Americans died in this terrible war. After the war ended in 1865, three constitutional amendments were passed to protect the rights of African Americans.

I'm sorry it took so long, my friend.

ABRAHAM LINCOLN

13TH AMENDMENT

Better late than never, sir!

The 13th Amendment ended slavery. The 14th gave equal protection under the law to all. The 15th Amendment gave African American men the right to vote.

Still many local governments discriminated against African Americans. State laws were passed that allowed segregation. African Americans were denied the right to stay in certain hotels. They were told to sit in the back of buses when traveling. They couldn't even eat in the same restaurants as white customers.

While African Americans never stopped dreaming of liberty, it took time to become a reality. Thanks to people like Dr. Martin Luther King Jr., the Civil Rights Act of 1964 became law. This act stopped discrimination on the basis of color, national origin, race, religion, or gender. The act also ended discrimination in hotels and restaurants.

DR. MARTIN LUTHER KING JR.

I have a dream today!

RING THE BELL

The Liberty Bell is a famous symbol of American independence. The bell got its name in 1837 when the American Anti-Slavery Society began using it as a symbol. The name came from the writing on the bell that reads: "Proclaim Liberty throughout all the Land unto all the Inhabitants thereof."

In 1865, a young French sculptor named Frederic Auguste Bartholdi was invited to a dinner party. The host of the gathering was writer and professor Edouard de Laboulaye. Talk at the party centered on the United States, and how France admired American independence.

Several years passed, but Bartholdi did not forget the idea. In 1871, he visited America. When his ship arrived in New York, he spotted a tiny island in the harbor. On that island, he imagined a magnificent statue rising to greet visitors to the New World.

By 1875, Bartholdi had made a small model of the planned statue. It would be known as the Statue of Liberty. Now came the hardest part. He needed to raise the money to build the statue.

Very nice, Mr. Bartholdi, but she is so small.

Will anyone be able to see tiny Lady Liberty from New York Harbor?

Good grief.

Eleven years later, on October 25, 1886, the Statue of Liberty was finished. Lady Liberty became a welcome sight to immigrants. Her torch lit the way as they passed through the immigration station on Ellis Island.

immigrant — someone who comes from one country to live permanently in a new country

I have completed my life's dream.

MEASURING LADY LIBERTY

The Statue of Liberty has some amazing statistics:

- The Statue of Liberty is more than 305 feet (93 meters) tall from the base of the pedestal to the tip of the torch.

- Lady Liberty's face is more than 8 feet (2.4 meters) tall.

- The statue weighs 450,000 pounds (204,117 kilograms).

- The copper skin of the Statue of Liberty is thinner than two pennies.

THE FOUR FREEDOMS

On January 6, 1941, President Franklin D. Roosevelt gave a memorable State of the Union Address. This landmark speech on liberty was known afterward as "The Four Freedoms."

Four freedoms are only a start. I've got plenty more!

FRANKLIN D. ROOSEVELT

Roosevelt was concerned that America could be pulled into war with Germany in the near future. He spoke about how the American model of liberty should be extended throughout the world.

UNITED STATES

In his speech, Roosevelt noted that four freedoms should be shared by people everywhere in the world.

Freedom of speech and expression.

Freedom from want.

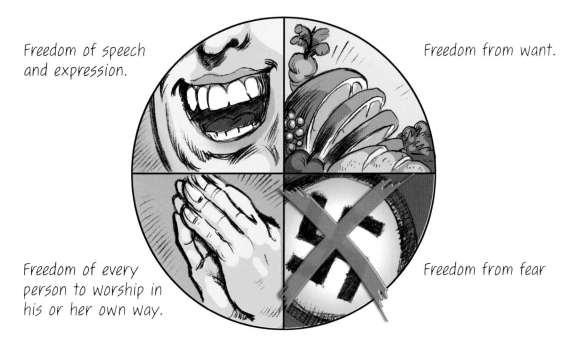

Freedom of every person to worship in his or her own way.

Freedom from fear

The ideas behind the Four Freedoms became part of a personal mission for First Lady Eleanor Roosevelt. They inspired her to present the Universal Declaration of Human Rights in 1948. This declaration has been translated into more languages than any other document in the world.

. . . The advent of a world in which human beings shall enjoy freedom of speech and belief and freedom from fear and want has been proclaimed the highest aspiration of the common people . . .

ELEANOR ROOSEVELT

For people to have liberty, they must be free to speak, think, and act without fear of punishment. Sadly, even today some people still don't have those rights. In many countries, people live under severe government control.

THE WORLD

Due to an unstable government and overpopulation, thousands of people have been killed in the Darfur region of western Sudan since February 2003. Many call the military conflict in this region of Africa genocide. To keep the deaths a secret, the government is believed to have jailed witnesses and destroyed evidence.

Live from Darfur NEWS

genocide — to destroy a race of people on purpose

Sri Lanka is another nation under watch for human rights violations. As recently as 2007, the government was accused of murder, police torture, and kidnapping. There are also reports of children being forced to become soldiers.

The 1989 Tiananmen Square Massacre is a forbidden topic in the People's Republic of China. Hundreds of people died while protesting strict government control. But censorship and fear of going to jail prevent the Chinese news media from talking about the massacre. Even Internet sites are censored regarding the topic.

But there are stories of hope. After World War II, the Berlin Wall divided East and West Germany. In 1989, the Berlin Wall was torn down. For the first time in 28 years, free travel between East and West Germany was allowed.

Each time a person stands up for what is right, progress is made across the globe. Without liberty, no other human dreams are possible.

The liberty that Americans enjoy should never be taken for granted. Liberty as a concept doesn't stop changing over time. Americans must avoid the loss of individual freedoms.

With each passing year, new technology threatens personal freedoms. Privacy can be invaded and our liberty compromised. The Internet allows access to the world. But it also can be used to find out personal information about the user.

After the 9/11 terrorist attacks, the U.S. Congress passed a law known as the Patriot Act. Cell phone records, public library records, and other private information could be reviewed to search for terrorists. The Patriot Act was passed to help keep Americans safe.

The Founding Fathers helped the colonies fight the first battles for American liberty. Leaders such as Jefferson, Washington, Adams, and Franklin knew the cost to gain liberty would be high. But they also knew the chance to have liberty was well worth the price.

TIME LINE

500 B.C. — The concept of liberty takes root in ancient Rome.

500 B.C.

1215 — In England, the Magna Carta says the king must obey the law, just like everyone else.

1215

1791 — The first 10 amendments, known as the Bill of Rights, are added to the U.S. Constitution.

1791

1789 — Writings about liberty by Montesquieu, Rousseau, and Voltaire lead to the French Revolution.

1789

1865 — The 13th Amendment to the Constitution ends slavery in the United States.

1865

1886 — France presents the United States with the gift of the Statue of Liberty.

1886

1689 — John Locke's *Two Treatises of Government* is published. This book later inspires Thomas Jefferson while writing the Declaration of Independence.

1689

1775 — The American Revolutionary War begins. Colonists fight for freedom from Great Britain.

1775

1776 — The Declaration of Independence is presented in Philadelphia to the Second Continental Congress.

1776

1920 — Women are given the right to vote with the passage of the 19th Amendment.

1920

1964 — Congress passes the Civil Rights Act. This act outlaws discrimination on the basis of color, national origin, race, religion, or gender.

1964

GLOSSARY

amendment (uh-MEND-muhnt) — a change made to a law or a legal document

anarchy (AN-ur-kee) — a situation with no order and no one in control

assembly (uh-SEM-blee) — a meeting of lots of people

censorship (SEN-suhr-ship) — the removal of something that is thought to be harmful or offensive to the public

citizen (SI-tuh-zuhn) — a member of a country or state who has the right to live there

class (KLAS) — a group of people in society with a similar way of life or range of income

democracy (di-MAH-kruh-see) — a form of government in which people can choose their leaders

discriminate (dis-KRI-muh-nayt) — to treat people unfairly because of their skin color or class

genocide (JEN-oh-side) — to destroy a race of people on purpose

immigrant (IM-uh-gruhnt) — someone who comes from one country to live permanently in another country

indivisible (in-duh-VIS-uh-buhl) — not able to be divided or broken into pieces

jury (JU-ree) — a group of people at a trial that decides if someone is guilty of a crime

monarchy (MON-ahr-kee) — a system of government in which the ruler is a king or queen

READ MORE

Gorman, Jacqueline Laks. *What Are Your Basic Rights?*
Know Your Government. Pleasantville, N.Y.: Weekly Reader
Books, 2008.

O'Donnell, Liam. *Democracy.* Cartoon Nation. Mankato, Minn.:
Capstone Press, 2008.

Peterson, Christine. *The U.S. Constitution.* Cartoon Nation.
Mankato, Minn.: Capstone Press, 2009.

Rees, Peter. *Liberty: Blessing or Burden?* Shockwave.
New York: Children's Press, 2008.

Woolf, Alex. *Democracy.* Systems of Government. Milwaukee:
World Almanac Library, 2006.

INTERNET SITES

FactHound offers a safe, fun way to find educator-approved
Internet sites related to this book.

Here's what you do:

1. Visit *www.facthound.com*
2. Choose your grade level.
3. Begin your search.

This book's ID number is 9781429623407.

FactHound will fetch the best sites for you!

INDEX

amendments, 16–17, 18, 28, 29
anarchy, 5
Antoinette, Marie, 15

Bartholdi, Frederic Auguste, 20–21
Berlin Wall, 25
Bill of Rights, 16–17, 28

Civil Rights Act of 1964, 19, 29

Darfur, 24
Declaration of Independence, 13, 29
discrimination, 19, 29

English Bill of Rights, 11

Four Freedoms, 22–23
Franklin, Benjamin, 12, 27
freedom, 5, 6, 7, 8, 9, 16, 18, 22–23, 25, 26, 29
   of religion, 5, 7, 16, 19, 23, 29
   of speech, 5, 7, 16, 23, 24

George III, King, 12

Jefferson, Thomas, 13, 27, 29

King, Dr. Martin Luther, Jr., 19

Libertas, 9
liberty
   types of, 5, 6–7
Liberty Bell, 19

Locke, John, 13, 29
Louis XVI, King, 15

Madison, James, 14
Magna Carta, 11, 28
Middle Ages, 10–11
Montesquieu, Charles, 14

Patriot Act, 27
Pledge of Allegiance, 4

rights, 5, 6, 7, 8, 10, 11, 13, 15, 16–17, 18, 19, 23, 24, 28, 29
   to assemble, 7, 16
   to bear arms, 16
   to vote, 6, 18, 29
Rome, 7, 8–9, 10, 28
Roosevelt, Eleanor, 23
Roosevelt, Franklin D., 22–23
Rousseau, Jean-Jacques, 14

slavery, 8–9, 18, 19, 28
Sri Lanka, 24
Statue of Liberty, 4, 20–21, 28

Tiananmen Square Massacre, 25

Universal Declaration of Human Rights, 23
U.S. Constitution, 14, 16, 17, 18, 28

Voltaire, 15